REMARKABLE

PEOPLE

Warren
Buffett

by Tamar Lupo

Published by Weigl Publishers Inc.
350 5th Avenue, Suite 3304, PMB 6G
New York, NY 10118-0069

Website: www.weigl.com

Library of Congress Cataloging-in-Publication Data

Lupo, Tamar.
  Warren Buffett / Tamar Lupo.
      p. cm. -- (Remarkable people)
  Includes index.
   ISBN 978-1-59036-651-6 (hard cover : alk. paper) -- ISBN 978-1-59036-652-3 (soft
cover : alk. paper)
   1. Buffett, Warren--Juvenile literature. 2. Capitalists and financiers--United States--
Biography--Juvenile literature. 3. Stockbrokers--United States--Biography--Juvenile
literature. I. Title.
  HG172.B84L87 2008
  332.6092--dc22
  [B]
                                    2006039442

Printed in the United States of America
1 2 3 4 5 6 7 8 9 0 11 10 09 08 07

Editor: Leia Tait
Design: Terry Paulhus

Cover: Warren Buffett is a wealthy investor who is well known for giving his money
to help others.

Contents

Who Is Warren Buffett?

Warren Buffett is an investor. He earns money by buying and selling **stocks**. Warren is the **Chief Executive Officer** of a company called Berkshire Hathaway. Warren **invests** Berkshire's money in businesses he believes will earn money in the future. Through these investments, he has helped make Berkshire Hathaway one of the largest and richest companies in the world. He has also become one of the world's wealthiest people. Warren is well known for using his money to help others. He is an example to many people in the business world and beyond.

> *"I think an example is the best thing you can leave behind."*

Growing Up

Warren Edward Buffett was born in Omaha, Nebraska, on August 30, 1930. His mother, Leila, worked at home raising Warren and his sisters, Doris and Bertie. His father, Howard, was a businessman who owned his own investment company. He also worked in government. As a boy, Warren was much like Howard. He was fascinated by money and business. He was very good at math. At a young age, Warren was able to calculate large sums in his head, without having to work them out on paper.

When he was 6 years old, Warren had his first business idea. He bought packs of chewing gun and soda pop from this grandparents' grocery store. Then he re-sold the items to people in his neighborhood, bringing them door-to-door. He sold each item for a few cents more than he had paid. From this experience, Warren learned about **profit**. He was earning money while other children his age were playing with toys.

■ Today, more than 800,000 people live in Omaha. It is Nebraska's largest city.

Get to Know Nebraska

FLAG

BIRD
Western Meadowlark

FLOWER
Goldenrod

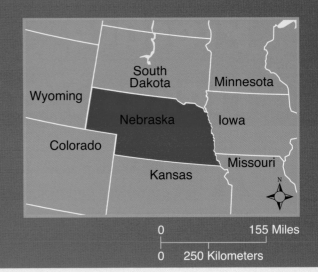

Wyoming
South Dakota
Minnesota
Nebraska
Iowa
Colorado
Kansas
Missouri

0		155 Miles
0	250 Kilometers	

In 1867, Nebraska became the 37th state.

Nebraska is near the center of the United States. It is bordered by Iowa, Colorado, Kansas, Missouri, South Dakota, and Wyoming.

The Missouri River appears on Nebraska's state flag.

Lincoln is the capital city of Nebraska. The state government meets in the capitol building there.

The white-tailed deer is one of Nebraska's official animals.

Think about it!

Warren first became interested in business while growing up in Nebraska. Think about the place where you live. What types of jobs do most people have? Are they farmers, bankers, scientists, or entertainers? Research a job that interests you. Is there a way you might become involved in this field right now?

Practice Makes Perfect

At age 11, Warren made his first investment. He bought some stocks in a company called Cities Service. These stocks earned Warren a small amount of money. He earned more money from a job delivering newspapers. By the time he was 14, Warren had saved $1,200. He used this money to buy 40 acres (16 hectares) of Nebraska farmland. Warren allowed farmers to use the land in return for a fee. He also earned money from pinball machines he and a friend placed in local barbershops.

Warren graduated from high school at the age of 17. For the next few years, he studied business. Warren spent two years at the Wharton Business School in Pennsylvania. In 1949, he returned to Omaha to finish his studies at the University of Nebraska.

■ Nebraska farmland is some of the richest in the world. Much of it is used for growing corn.

Warren earned his business **degree** in 1950. He continued his studies at Columbia University in New York City. In 1951, Warren earned an advanced degree in **economics** from Columbia Business School.

For the next three years, Warren worked at his father's investment company. There, he helped clients invest their money. Warren learned a great deal about investing from this experience. In 1956, he started his own investment company. It was called the Buffett Partnership. The company quickly became very successful.

■ Columbia University is known for the design of its buildings. Many, such as Low Memorial Library, were made to resemble ancient Greek structures.

Key Events

In 1962, the Buffett Partnership invested in a company called Berkshire Hathaway. Over time, Warren bought so many stocks that he gained control of the company. In 1967, Warren used Berkshire Hathaway to begin investing in **insurance**. He and the company made a great deal of money from these investments. By 1969, Warren closed the Buffett Partnership to focus entirely on Berkshire Hathaway.

Over the next few years, Warren invested the money he made from Berkshire Hathaway into many large companies. These included Coca Cola™, American Express, and the Government Employees Insurance Company (GEICO). All of these investments were very successful. They helped make Berkshire Hathaway one of the largest **holding companies** in the world. Warren became very rich and well known. His success earned him the nickname "the **Oracle** of Omaha."

■ By 1980, Warren had earned almost $140 million.

Thoughts from Warren

Warren's interest in business made him a successful investor. Here are some of the things he has said about his life and work.

Warren learns how important every action is in business.

"It takes 20 years to build a reputation and five minutes to ruin it. If you think about that, you'll do things differently."

Warren believes he has been lucky in life.

"I was born with the right skills, in the right place, at the right time."

Warren tries to live like everyone else, even though he is very rich.

"Money aside, there is very little difference between you and me in terms of lifestyle. I eat simple meals. I drive a regular car. I make decisions, and, yes, I, too, make mistakes."

Warren believes people can achieve important successes in ordinary tasks.

"It is not necessary to do extraordinary things to get extraordinary results."

Warren creates an investment plan.

"We simply attempt to be fearful when others are greedy and to be greedy only when others are fearful."

Warren gives advice to new investors.

"Never invest in a business you cannot understand."

What Is an Investor?

An investor is someone who spends money with the hope of making a profit in the future. Some investors buy **real estate** that they hope will become more valuable over time. Others, such as Warren Buffett, buy and sell stocks and **shares**. This gives buyers part ownership of companies. As the companies make money, they become more valuable. The value of their stocks increase, and investors make money.

Stocks and shares can be purchased on the **stock market** or directly from a company. When purchasing shares, most investors think about the future. They buy shares of a company and hold onto these shares for many years. If the shares increase in value, investors can make a profit by selling them at a higher price than they paid for them.

■ The New York Stock Exchange is the oldest and largest stock market in the United States.

Investors 101

Donald Trump (1946–)

Field: Real Estate
Career: Donald Trump began his career working with his father in the construction business. There, Trump learned how to make professional business deals. Later, he began investing in New York real estate. He quickly became successful. Today, the Trump Organization owns many well-known buildings in the United States, such as Trump Tower in New York City and Trump Plaza in New Jersey. Trump has written many popular books about his experiences in business. In 2004, he created a television reality show called *The Apprentice*. It quickly became one of the most successful shows on television.

Zoe Cruz (1955–)

Field: Investment Banking
Career: Zoe Cruz began her career as an investment banker. Investment bankers help companies find investors. They also help clients make investment decisions. In 1982, Cruz began working at an investment bank called Morgan Stanley. By 1990, she was involved in managing the company. Over the next few years, Cruz became a successful **stockbroker**. In 2005, she was made a co-president of Morgan Stanley. The firm is one of the largest investment banks in the United States. In 2006, *Forbes* magazine named Cruz one of the 10 most powerful women in the world.

Abigail Johnson (1962–)

Field: Mutual Funds
Career: As a young woman, Abigail Johnson studied business at Harvard University. In 1988, she began working full time at Fidelity Investments. Her grandfather, Edward Johnson II, started Fidelity in 1946. Today, it is the largest mutual fund company in the United States. In 2001, Johnson became president of Fidelity's mutual funds branch. Today, she shares control of the company with her father. In 2006, Johnson was among the 30 richest people in the world.

Bill Gates (1955–)

Field: Computer **Software**
Career: Bill Gates began programming computers when he was 13 years old. After studying at Harvard University, Gates began his own computer company in 1975. It was called Microsoft **Corporation**. Today, Microsoft is the most used computer software in the world. Gates has earned billions of dollars from his product. With this money, he has become a successful investor. Each year, Gates invests billions into Microsoft and other companies, such as the Canadian National Railway and Berkshire Hathaway. Gates gives a great deal of his own money to **charity** groups around the world.

The Stock Ticker

A stock ticker is a tool that prints stock prices on long strips of paper called ticker tape. It was invented in 1867. The ticker printed symbols that were used to identify different companies. Stock prices for the companies were printed beside the symbols. Stock tickers were named for the ticking noise they made while printing. Today, large television screens display the symbols and prices that once appeared on ticker tape. The screens are sometimes still called stock tickers.

Influences

Warren had two **mentors** early in his life—his father, Howard, and his teacher, Dr. Benjamin Graham. Howard was a stockbroker in Omaha. He owned his own investment business, called Buffett-Falk & Co. Warren worked there from 1951 to 1954, after finishing business school. Like his father, Warren bought and sold stocks and bonds on behalf of clients. He learned a great deal about investing during this time.

Howard served in the U.S. government. In 1942, Howard was chosen to represent the state of Nebraska in the U.S. **House of Representatives**. There, Howard was known for promoting libertarianism. This is a belief that people should be free to think and do what they please as long as they do not limit other people's freedoms. This taught Warren to be an independent thinker. He learned to trust his own judgement when making investment decisions, instead of following everyone else.

■ The House of Representatives meets inside the House Chamber of the Capitol building in Washington, DC.

Dr. Benjamin Graham was another of Warren's mentors. Dr. Graham was a well-known investor. He taught business at Columbia University, where Warren was his student. Warren was the only student to earn an A+ grade in one of Dr. Graham's classes. A few years after Warren completed his studies, Dr. Graham hired him to work at his investment company. It was called the Graham-Newman Corporation, and was located on Wall Street in New York City. Warren worked there from 1954 to 1956. He learned investment skills that later helped him become successful.

WALL STREET

Wall Street is a street in the lower Manhattan area of New York City. It was named for a wall that once surrounded the island of Manhattan. Today, Wall Street is the center of the U.S. stock market. It is home to the New York Stock Exchange and some of the most important banks in the United States, such as the Federal Reserve Bank of New York. This bank is the first to act on government decisions about how money is used in the United States. Often, the name "Wall Street" is used to refer to the entire U.S. investment community.

■ The Charging Bull statue, also called the Wall Street Bull, is a well-known symbol of the U.S. financial district. It is located in Bowling Green Park near Wall Street.

Overcoming Obstacles

Warren faced many difficulties early in his life. He was born in 1930, the year after the Great Depression began. This was a 10-year period when money and jobs were scarce in the United States. Warren's father had a job at a bank, but because of the depression, he did not earn much money. Harsh weather made the situation worse. There was very little rain, and farmers could not grow healthy crops. Warren's family often did not have enough food. His mother sometimes skipped meals so that Warren's father had enough to eat. This had a great impact on Warren. He became fascinated with money and often wished to be rich. One of his favorite books to read at this time was called *One Thousand Ways to Make $1,000*. Warren began searching for ways that he could earn money.

■ The Great Depression began on October 29, 1929, when prices on the U.S. stock market suddenly dropped. Panicked businessmen crowded Wall Street hoping to recover their money from the banks.

When Warren decided to have a career in business, he knew he faced some challenges. Like many people, Warren did not enjoy making speeches in public. He knew that to be successful in business, he needed to be comfortable speaking in front of others. To improve his skills, Warren took a course on public speaking. This made him a more confident speaker. He even began teaching investment classes at the University of Omaha in 1951.

■ Warren speaks in front of large audiences at media events. He often travels to schools to speak to large groups of business students.

Achievements and Successes

Many people believe that Warren is the most successful investor in history. At the start of 2006, he was worth more than $40 billion. For the sixth year in a row, *Forbes* magazine listed him as the second-richest person in the world. Despite his success, Warren leads a simple life. He continues to live in the same Omaha house he bought in 1958.

Warren enjoys sharing his knowledge with others. Every year, he writes a report on Berkshire Hathaway's activities. The reports are written in the form of a letter to his clients and coworkers. They are read by many important business leaders and investors. In them, Warren shares his personal experiences and investment advice. In 1996, many of these letters were collected in a book called *The Essays of Warren Buffett: Lessons for Corporate America.*

■ In 2001, Warren received a can of "Buffett Green" paint. The color, which is named for him, is made to match U.S. money.

Warren's success has allowed him to help people in many ways. In the 1960s, Warren and his wife started a charity called the Buffett Foundation. After Susan died in 2004, it was renamed the Susan Thompson Buffett Foundation. The charity gives money to U.S. students who would not otherwise be able to attend school. It also provides money for women's programs throughout the United States.

In June 2006, Warren announced a plan to give away most of his personal fortune to charity. He divided $6 billion between the Susan Thompson Buffett Foundation and three other charities run by his children. Warren then gave Berkshire Hathaway stocks worth about $30 billion to the Bill and Melinda Gates Foundation. This is the largest sum of money given to charity in history.

THE BILL AND MELINDA GATES FOUNDATION

Bill and Melinda Gates created the Bill and Melinda Gates Foundation in 2000. The charity works to improve lives around the world. It is guided by the belief that every life has equal value. The foundation works to end hunger and poverty in the world's poorest countries. It gives money to help scientists find cures for serious diseases. It also seeks to improve education in the United States, by providing programs for children in need. To learn more about the Bill and Melinda Gates Foundation, visit the foundation's website at **www.gatesfoundation.org**.

Write a Biography

A person's life story can be the subject of a book. This kind of book is called a biography. Biographies describe the lives of remarkable people, such as those who have achieved great success or have done important things to help others. These people may be alive today or they may have lived many years ago. Reading a biography can help you learn more about a remarkable person.

At school, you might be asked to write a biography. First, decide who you want to write about. You can choose a business hero, such as Warren Buffett, or any other person you find interesting. Then, find out if your library has any books about this person. Learn as much as you can about him or her. Write down the key events in this person's life. What was this person's childhood like? What has he or she accomplished? What are his or her goals? What makes this person special or unusual?

A concept web is a useful research tool. Read the questions in the following concept web. Answer the questions in your notebook. Your answers will help you write your biography.

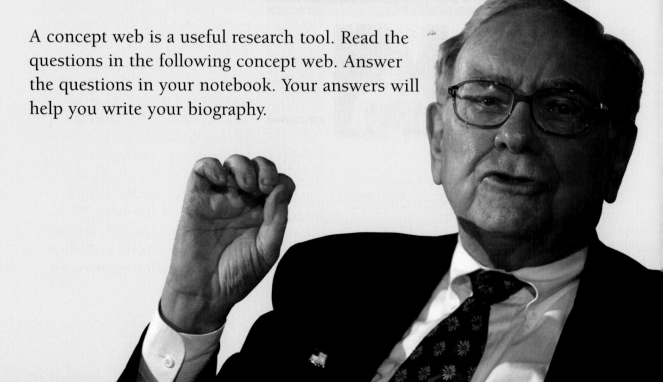

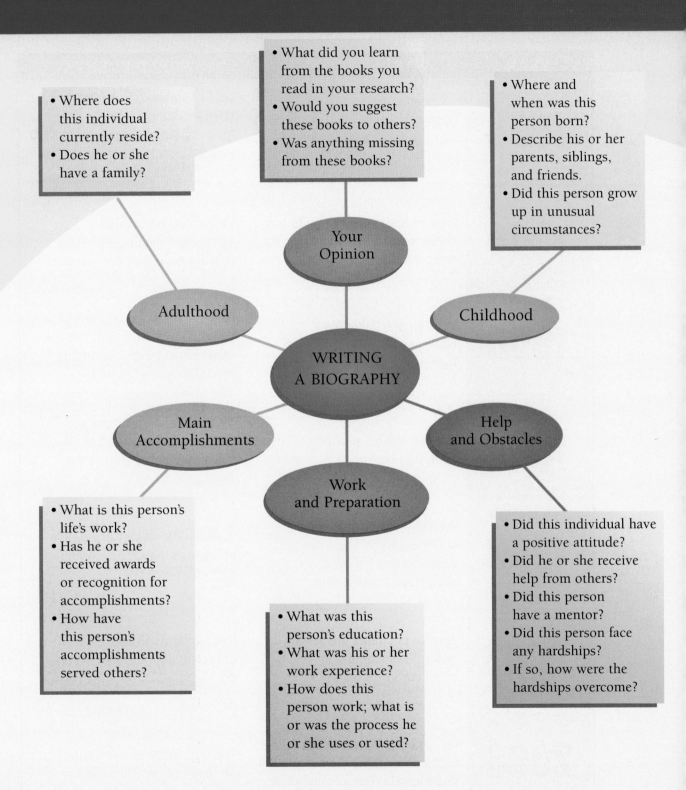

- Where does this individual currently reside?
- Does he or she have a family?

- What did you learn from the books you read in your research?
- Would you suggest these books to others?
- Was anything missing from these books?

- Where and when was this person born?
- Describe his or her parents, siblings, and friends.
- Did this person grow up in unusual circumstances?

Your Opinion

Adulthood

Childhood

WRITING A BIOGRAPHY

Main Accomplishments

Help and Obstacles

Work and Preparation

- What is this person's life's work?
- Has he or she received awards or recognition for accomplishments?
- How have this person's accomplishments served others?

- What was this person's education?
- What was his or her work experience?
- How does this person work; what is or was the process he or she uses or used?

- Did this individual have a positive attitude?
- Did he or she receive help from others?
- Did this person have a mentor?
- Did this person face any hardships?
- If so, how were the hardships overcome?

Timeline

YEAR	WARREN BUFFETT	WORLD EVENTS
1930	Warren is born in Omaha, Nebraska, on August 30, 1930.	On December 2, President Herbert Hoover asks the U.S. government to provide up to $150 million to create jobs during the Great Depression.
1944	Warren uses his savings to buy some farmland in Nebraska. He rents the land to farmers.	World War II continues. Countries from Europe, Asia, and the Americas are involved.
1956	Warren starts his own company, called the Buffett Partnership.	In September, the first telephone cable across the Atlantic Ocean begins operating. It connects Great Britain to Canada.
1965	Warren and his partners take control of Berkshire Hathaway.	Silver is no longer used in dimes and quarters after the U.S. government passes the Coinage Act.
1988	Warren buys his first stocks in Coca-Cola™. This later becomes one his most successful investments.	In April, Microsoft Corporation becomes the world's leading software provider.
2001	Warren becomes the second-richest person in the world.	George W. Bush becomes president of the United States on January 20.
2006	On June 25, Warren gives stocks worth about $30 billion to the Bill and Melinda Gates Foundation.	The population of the United States reaches 300 million.

Further Research

How can I find out more about Warren Buffett?

Most libraries have computers that connect to a database for searching for information. If you input a key word, you will be provided with a list of books in the library that contain information on that topic. Non-fiction books are arranged numerically, using their call number. Fiction books are organized alphabetically by the author's last name.

Websites

To learn more about Warren Buffett, visit www.berkshirehathaway.com

To learn more about investing, visit www.younginvestor.com/kids/

Words to Know

charity: a fund for helping people in need

Chief Executive Officer (CEO): the highest-ranking person in a company or corporation, responsible for its overall management

corporation: a group of people who act as a single unit in order to carry out business

degree: a title given to a student upon completion of his or her studies

economics: the science that studies how money, goods, and services are created and used

holding companies: companies that are created to own and control other companies

House of Representatives: the lawmaking body of the U.S. Congress

insurance: the business of providing protection against loss or damage in return for a fee

invests: spends money in order to make more money in the future

mentors: wise and trusted teachers

mutual funds: sums of money from many investors that are managed by companies or investment advisors

oracle: in ancient times, a priest or priestess who was believed to speak with the gods

profit: the money gained from something

real estate: property made up of buildings and land

shares: portions of a corporation's property that are divided equally

software: the programs used by a computer

stockbroker: someone who handles orders to buy and sell stocks

stock market: where stocks and shares are bought and sold

stocks: the shares of a company or corporation

Index

DATE DUE
